The King's Baker

The King's Baker

A TALE OF A JOURNEY TO INNOVATIVE LEADERSHIP

By Robert Davidovich Ed.D. and John Koehn Ph.D.

Published By Julian John Publishing
6650 W State St Unit D #232
Wauwatosa WI 53213

Special Note: This edition of "The King's Baker, A Tale of a Journey to Innovative Leadership" is designed to provide information to our readers. It is sold with the understanding that the publisher is not engaged to render any type of legal or other professional advice. No warranties or guarantees are expressed or implied by the publisher's choice to include any of the content in this volume. Neither the publisher nor the authors shall be liable for any damages, including, but not limited to, special, incidental, consequential or other damages.

Printed in the United States of America

Publisher's Cataloging-in-Publication
(Provided by Quality Books, Inc.)

    Davidovich, Robert.
       The kings baker : a tale of a journey to innovative
       leadership / by Robert Davidovich and John Koehn.
       p. cm.
    ISBN-13: 978-0-98216268-2
    ISBN-10: 0-9821626-8-5

    1. Leadership. I. Koehn, John, 1935- II. Title.
    HD57.7.D38 2011   658.4

            QBI11-600051

Dedication

TO: GERDA AND RUTH

Thank you for being at our sides. You provide the meaning for our lives and our work.

ALSO, it is with deep appreciation that we thank the many family members, friends, and colleagues who gave us feedback and encouragement during the development of this book.
Your support led us on.

We would like to extend a special thank you for the wonderful insights of **JACKSON V. PARKER** and his contributions to the questions that end the epilogue.

WE ARE GRATEFUL.

Contents

Prologue 9

The Kings Baker 13

Epilogue 97

About The Authors 105

Prologue

THE KING'S BAKER: A TALE OF A JOURNEY TO INNOVATIVE LEADERSHIP

Today's certainties are death, taxes... and in business, the fact that someone is going to come along with a game-changing product or service that makes the existing norm obsolete. In today's world, change is accelerating and pressing in on us all the time. How we approach it is crucial to our continued organizational success. Changes in our external environment cause us to ask questions such as: What does this change mean for my organization? Is it significant enough that we need to alter what we do, or should we let it pass and stay the course? Does responding mean that we tweak what we are already doing, or do we need to come up with a new approach? How leaders answer these questions is often the difference between their organization riding a wave of success or getting drawn down to the bottom in an undertow.

The stakes for answering these questions are much higher now. This is true because it is not only the accelerated pace of change that compresses reaction time, but the fact that small, seemingly insignificant occurrences can turn the landscape of success upside down overnight. Your business or organization can be doing all the right things and in what seems to be an instant, the ground rules of success can change – what was once your strength may become your weakness. Just think of what digital photograph caused for Kodak, or what 9/11 meant to government intelligence, or what social networking means for political action and organizing movements. Knowing when to abandon one successful life cycle for a new, untested one is an essential new skill for leaders of all organizations. But how does one know when to leap?

The 14th century was chosen as the setting for our story to emphasize the fact that people have been struggling with this challenge for a very long time – in fact, since the beginning of time. However, while the process of renewal and transformation remains constant, the present response time for leaders is much more compressed. The metaphor in this book is designed to provide a description of, and an emotional connection to, the phenomenon of change leaders of all organizations face today: When is it time to help the organization get better at what it does? And when is it time to help it become different? For leaders, answering these questions may mean not always following conventional business wisdom – instead, setting off on the path of self-discovery.

Our lead character Bernard's experience is metaphoric and can help each of us reflect on old life cycles of leadership that are reaching the end of their effectiveness while also allowing us to assess emerging organizational needs and corresponding new leadership attributes. In this new world of leadership, messes become important opportunities for they are the very thing that can start us on the path of self-discovery. Traveling on this path leads to an enhanced capacity to understand change and its meaning for your world. The journey involves much unlearning and relearning on your part. Some of what you now believe about leadership may need to be reflected upon and re-evaluated.

As you read this book, jot down notes, key insights or "aha's" that you discover as Bernard "transforms" into his new leadership style. This may allow you to connect factors or things you are experiencing in your current leadership role that may be similar to those of Bernard's experience. We hope reading and using this book will be helpful as you deal with the intersection of new and old life cycles–personally and organizationally. Enjoy the journey.

– BOB AND JOHN

One

Long ago King Louie and Queen Marie were the gracious and benevolent rulers of the small kingdom of Fredonia. Their people were happy and prosperous. Fredonia was a wonderful place to live and work. The air was fresh and no social ills or moral dilemmas could be found. Its people learned to strike a healthy balance between work and leisure. But, most of all, Fredonians were known for their love of fine baked goods.

This reputation was a direct result of King Louie's love of fine baked goods. He supported this love by regarding bakers as the most esteemed and elevated members of his society. Laws and decrees issued by the King most often had something to do with encouraging the creation and consumption of baked goods that delighted the King and his people. Oh, King Louie loved his baked goods – and his physique showed it – although no one would tell him that he looked anything but extremely fit. This, of course, was because the people of Fredonia shared the King's passion and possessed similar "fit" physiques.

Of all the bakers, one stood out in favor with the King. He stood out so much that everyone referred to Baker Bernard as "The King's Baker."

Bernard's baked goods were exquisite. He had learned his craft well, graduating at the top of his class at the baker's guild. His legend grew as he won the King's annual baking competition 10 years in a row. His torte, baked exclusively for the competition, was considered heavenly. It was a rare and savory taste that made one salivate in anticipation and desire to do cartwheels at the first bite. It was so good that cartwheels would have actually been performed – if the Fredonians could have gotten their bodies to move that gingerly.

It was not just good training that helped Bernard

become the King's Baker. No one had a greater sense of just what would please the King's palette than he. Bernard internalized the rules for baking success better than anyone – use top ingredients and guard your recipes. Most importantly, he hired the best and trained them well within a tight system of production overseen by a strong chain of command. Bernard ran his system of baking with the complete authority of a king in his own right – ruling over a well-established and highly respected bakery.

Fredonia had many fine bakers who were highly thought of and whose baked goods were enjoyed – but none achieved Bernard's level of success. Oh, other bakers tried to unseat Bernard as the top baker in Fredonia, but none could match his knowledge, skill and system of production.

One year the King's daughter, Princess Madeline, celebrated her 18th birthday. Princess Madeline was a truly lovely young lady with great charm and grace who was greatly admired and loved by her subjects. She was also known to be a strong-willed, independent child who did not always see the world in the same way as the King. While the King was quite happy and content with the world as it was defined within the borders of Fredonia, the princess longed for new experiences and excitement found beyond the borders.

That year rumors began to circulate around the kingdom that the King was afraid his daughter may desire to spread her wings and leave Fredonia. To appease Princess Madeline and to honor her birthday, some speculated that the King would give her a significant hand in judging the annual baking competition. After all, what greater love could the King show than to share some control of his beloved baking competition with his only child?

Bernard heard the rumors, yet he paid them no heed. He had not reached the status of King's Baker by paying attention to rumors or fads. Why change the tried and true? His torte was to die for. This year, as with the past ten, he would enter his famous, award-winning torte in the competition.

As time for the competition approached, everyone

in Bernard's bakery knew what to do. With incredible dedication every baker's assistant executed his or her part of the process with precision. The assistant in charge of flour knew just where to get the best flour; the same was true for the assistants in charge of eggs, sugar, and all of the ingredients. The recipe was known only in the memory of Bernard and once the ingredients arrived, he combined just the right amounts into his secret recipe. The assistants in charge of mixing, and those in charge of filling the pans, and those in charge of placing the pans in the ovens all did their job with great pride and skill. Bernard oversaw the production and closely watched the torte as it baked.

At just the right time – a time when Bernard perceived what only he could – the torte, emitting a fabulous aroma, was pulled from the oven, spontaneously stimulating wild applause and slaps on the back amongst the assistants. The kitchen would then fall silent as Bernard carefully crafted and skillfully assembled the layers of the torte. As if working with a canvas and brush, his finishing flare created a masterpiece. What about its flavor?

Everyone held his or her breath as Bernard stood poised with fork in hand over his final creation weighing just the right spot to extract a sample. The next moments seemed like an eternity as assistants looked for the slightest signs of reaction in Bernard's face. Finally, as a smile beamed across his face, Bernard would raise his arms to the heavens and shout, "Magnifique!" Absolute exuberance filled the room as relief gave way to joy and celebration. Bernard's reaction was all they needed to know, for if he was pleased with the torte then it surely would please the King and win the competition – once again.

The day everyone had impatiently waited a year for arrived with much anticipation and excitement. The annual baking competition was the highest of holidays in Fredonia. Bakers from all over the land gathered at the town square in a time-honored tradition. There they formed a procession that made its way through the crowded, winding streets toward the castle. All the bakers proudly displayed their creations to the crowd as the procession moved along.

Fredonians were high purveyors of etiquette, as well as pomp and circumstance, so it was only fitting that the most esteemed bakers brought up the rear of the procession – literally saving the best for last. The crowd showed its appreciation with cheers of approval that rose to a crescendo as Bernard slowly passed by with his torte raised above his head. People screamed out to him pleading for his acknowledgement and begged for the opportunity to inhale the aroma of his torte. It was these moments that Bernard lived for. The adulation he received at this competition elevated him to hero status, something he secretly found to be even more alluring than pleasing the King's palette. As he moved through the procession he felt invincible and as divine as any hero had ever felt. He was on top of the world.

The procession finally made its way through the castle gate and up to the King's courtyard. Tables that seemed to stretch for miles awaited the baked goods. Each piece was carefully arranged and documented for the judges. Judging was one of the most highly protected secrets in Fredonia. No one knew who the judges were, or for that matter, even how many there were. Some said it was only the King who judged. Some said it was the

King and Queen. Others said that it was the King's royal advisors. All anyone knew for sure was that the next day the top 10 winners were announced and small samples of each were made available to citizens on a first-in-line, first-served basis. The remainder of the baked goods was made available for the public to sample at will.

The winners were announced with great fanfare. All the bakers appeared before the King. Hearts pounded wildly as they held their breath hoping to hear their name announced. What an honor it was to hear your name announced as one of the top three bakers, then to step forward and have a medal placed around your neck and receive a grateful embrace from the King. The heartfelt cheers of the crowd ensured your bakery would be filled with customers for the next year.

For Bernard there was no such angst. He knew that he had a winning formula and knew that he had prepared it masterfully. Unlike the other bakers, he slept well the night before the winners were announced. To Bernard, the outcome was predictable and certain. Knowing what it takes to win ten years in a row, allowed him to remain calm, almost complacent as he waited to hear his name announced as the winner once again.

The morning of the announcement, citizens arose early and congregated with holiday-type good cheer in the castle's courtyard. People reacquainted with old friends and shared the latest neighborhood news. There was also a fair amount of wagering that took place on which bakers would be among the top three – though no one was foolish enough to bet against Bernard for the top award.

Finally, the King emerged on the balcony overlooking the courtyard, and the crowd fell silent. He greeted the crowd and extended heartfelt gratitude to the seventy-six bakers who had entered this year's competition. He commended the accomplishments of Fredonia's skilled bakers while marveling at the wonders they had created. Some in the crowd swore that they could still see bits of whipped cream and sugar in the King's beard. His smile and glow assured all that he had surely had a wonderful night of pleasure sampling the baked goods he had praised. He then worked his way down the stairway onto the platform that had been staged magnificently in the courtyard.

As the King read the list of winners, beginning with tenth place, the bakers waited with mixed emotions. While it was a great honor to hear your name in places ten through four, it also burst the bubble of hope each of these bakers had held to be one of the medal winners. The King then repositioned himself on the platform as he prepared for the final three names.

He announced that this year's third-place winner was Baker Jack, and second-place went to Baker Bernard.

The announcement was so unexpected that the collective gasp lingered to a point where no one heard the name of the first-place winner. Bernard found himself on the verge of collapse. It was as though his legs could not support him. He felt the blood drain from his head and the world began to spin. Several bakers standing next to him propped him up and assisted him toward the King to receive the second-place medal.

Two

All that he remembered about the remainder of that day was sitting in his kitchen staring at the second place medal in disbelief feeling numb and disoriented. He had no idea of how he made it through the crowd and back to his bakery – or who the winner was.

The next day as he sat again lamenting the results, his employees stopped in individually and in small groups to console him. Every one of them pointed out how unfair the results had been and that they were certain that it must have been some kind of mistake in judging. This consensus fostered the opinion that there was nothing wrong with the torte. In his mind, Bernard knew that the torte was well-prepared and up to the high standards that he had set over the years.

When the conversations turned to the competition's winner, Baker Sophie, cynicism reinforced the feeling of injustice. Baker Sophie was a middle-of-the-road baker who had only one top-ten finish to her resume. She seemed an incapable winner who must have gotten lucky ... or something. This whole competition had been some kind of fluke; an anomaly that would not be repeated anytime soon. From these types of conversations over the next few days, opinion became fact and a collective comfort arose around the belief that working just a little bit harder would surely compensate for what was referred to as "the great injustice." And so they did.

As time for the next year's competition approached, confidence in Bernard's bakery was high ... with just a touch of doubt underlying it. What if the same quirky judging was there this year? What if Sophie, or another baker, had some influence or favor with the judges? What if the information had been switched by someone and Bernard's torte had been mislabeled as Sophie's? In the end, everyone took solace in knowing that they had a proven, winning formula. Last year's competition had been a wake-up call. There would be no complacency this year, as everyone worked harder to prepare the torte.

As always, the assistant in charge of flour knew just where to get the best flour; the same was true for the assistants in charge of eggs, sugar, and all of the ingredients. The assistants in charge of mixing, those in charge of filling the pans, and those in charge of placing the pans in the ovens all put more effort and attention into their jobs this year. Bernard oversaw the production and closely watched the torte as it baked. At just the right time, the torte – emitting a familiar, fabulous aroma – was pulled from the oven. The kitchen again fell silent as Bernard put even more effort into skillfully assembling the layers of the torte. Then, everyone held his or her breath even longer than last year while Bernard stood poised with fork in hand over the final creation. The next moments seemed like an eternity as assistants looked for the slightest signs of reaction in Bernard's face. Finally, the intensity on his face eased slightly as his arms raised to the heavens and a modest "magnifique" was spoken. Instead of the usual exuberance, sighs of relief filled the room. Bernard's reaction was all they needed to know, for if he was pleased with the torte then it surely would please the King and win the competition – once again.

On the day of the competition the procession commenced with all of its rich tradition. It seemed strange and greatly uncomfortable for Bernard to not be in the position of final baker. As he glanced back occasionally he saw the glow on Sophie's face. He could not wait to end this strange year and return to his rightful position. Perhaps it was just a bit of bruised ego interfering, but as he moved along the route he had a hard time shaking the sense that the adulation from the crowd was not quite as strong as it should have been for a baker of his status.

Once in the courtyard, the baked goods were received and placed upon the tables. Bernard lingered just a bit, watching to make sure that his torte was properly labeled. Upon returning home, he ate dinner and prepared himself for bed. His usual night of restful confidence was replaced by some tossing and turning. Yet, in the morning he awoke and prepared for the announcement with the reassurance that this nightmarish year would become a fading memory when his name was again called as the winner of this year's competition.

The day of the announcement of the winners was as beautiful as ever. No one could even recall a day from the past when the weather had been anything short of spectacular for this occasion. As the King stood on the platform and began to read the list of winners starting with tenth place, the anxiety within Bernard, and all his assistants, began to grow. This feeling was not something with which Bernard was accustomed to dealing. As the announcement went on Bernard listened in a way that he had not in the past. This time he paid attention to the names ... seventh place, Baker Emily ... sixth place, Baker Will ... fifth place, Baker Kate ... fourth place, Baker Henry. Then in his time honored tradition, the King repositioned himself on the platform as he prepared for the final three names.

He announced that this year's third place winner was ... Baker Bernard. Bernard heard nothing after that as his head began to buzz and his body went numb. This year he stood without wavering and stepped forward to receive his medal with great indignation and resentment. This was a complete disgrace, and the medal would be discarded as soon as he found a suitable place to dispose of it.

Three

It took weeks for the shock that had reverberated through Fredonia to subside – the "King's Baker" was now the third-best baker. During that time, Bernard's disbelief at his fate was replaced by embarrassment. Eventually embarrassment gave way to anger, which evolved into a zealous focus on returning to the top so that what was rightfully his could be reclaimed.

During this time, life for the assistants at Bernard's bakery was awful. Bernard was sure that some aspect of his system must have broken down and failed. His obsession with finding the flaw created meetings searching for evidence of what went wrong that had the feel of an autopsy. Finding blame and pointing fingers at others soured the working conditions for all those under Bernard. Some assistants sought to protect their interests by developing speculation into "sound theories" about who was not doing his or her job – passing this information to Bernard in "confidential" conversations. Bernard's response to all of this was to lay down a mandate to everyone in no uncertain terms: *Everyone must get better at his or her job or else he or she would be fired!*

The year leading up to the next competition was a time of intense focus on improving the production of the torte. Every process was broken down and carefully scrutinized for areas to improve. Data about each aspect of the production process were analyzed. As the competition approached, Bernard's system of production had been refined and improved. Assistants were held accountable through improved supervision and more focused evaluations. Mistakes were not tolerated. Even farmers were aware of the need to grow better ingredients or be replaced by someone who could meet the higher standards required to be a supplier for Bernard's bakery.

As time for the competition approached, an edge of anxiety was felt by everyone in the bakery. As in the past every assistant did his or her job with precision, yet nervous trepidation replaced the once-felt confidence. The assistant in charge of flour analyzed data looking for where to get the very best flour; the same was true for the assistants in charge of eggs, sugar and all of the ingredients. Once the ingredients arrived, Bernard tested them for quality, and then combined just the right amounts into his secret recipe. The assistants in charge of mixing, and those in charge of filling the pans, and those in charge of placing the pans in the ovens all did their job with an improved skill. At just the right time – a time now prescribed to the second – the torte, emitting its familiar aroma and stimulating controlled restraint amongst the assistants, was pulled from the oven. The kitchen fell silent as Bernard precisely followed his written protocol for assembling the layers of the torte. He extracted a sample and ran tests on its content. Bernard examined the test data and then proclaimed the torte was ready. Not only was it ready, Bernard thought the new procedures brought his torte to a level of being the best he had ever created. Optimism filled the room as his reaction reassured everyone that the torte should win the competition.

In its rich tradition, the day of the competition commenced with the joyous fanfare of the bakers' procession. However, it was not joyous for Bernard as he begrudgingly lined up third baker from the end. It was with an increasingly deflated ego that he moved along the route, sensing that the adulation from the crowd was not nearly what he had grown accustomed to in his winning years.

Once in the courtyard, the baked goods were received and placed upon the tables. Bernard did not linger but returned quickly to the sanctuary of his home. He had a simple dinner and prepared himself for bed. His night was filled with tumultuous unrest. In the morning he awoke tired and stressed. He prepared for the announcement feeling far less confident. The old feeling of being in control of his destiny had faded. This time there was no great feeling of reassurance that his nightmarish two-year period would become a distant unpleasant memory.

The day of the announcement of the winners was as beautiful as ever. Yet, to Bernard the day seemed gloomy and foreboding. As the King positioned himself on the platform to read the list of winners, beginning with tenth place, the feeling within Bernard and all his assistants was unmistakable – fear had replaced anxiety. They all possessed a growing fear of failure. As the announcement went on Bernard listened in a way that he had not in the past – dreading what he might hear. This time as the fifth-place winner was announced Bernard's world came crashing down upon him. He and his "best ever" torte were now in that place. It was a place he could never have imagined for himself and his bakery just a few short years ago. For the first time, despair began to replace the zealous focus he had developed over the last year. Self-pity and hopelessness quickly set in. He was at a loss with no idea of what to do next.

Four

Bernard did not return to the bakery the next morning. Instead he left his home early after a sleepless night and began to walk by himself; wandering aimlessly through the Fredonian countryside. He did not want to run into people he knew, for he was too embarrassed about his tumble from the top to have to listen to awkward questions or disingenuous sympathy about his situation. Worst of all, he had applied everything he had ever learned about running a bakery in trying to regain his once-held status, and now he was further behind than ever. Everything he had learned had failed him.

As he walked along, kicking stones in the road, Bernard strained to find answers for what to do next.

The harder he tried to figure out what to do, the more frustrated he became. He had always been the one with answers in his bakery. He had always been the one to save a recipe or turn a potential disaster into something productive. He was the one everyone turned to in a crisis and now he was not answering the call. This was the hardest part of all for how could he lead his assistants if he did not have the answers? Perhaps his career as a baker was finished. Bernard began to contemplate changes he could make in his life... but all he knew was baking. Yet, how could he return and face the humiliation of the "King's Baker" being Fredonia's fifth-best baker?

After a while, Bernard looked up to find that he was walking on a narrow path through unfamiliar woods. He suddenly realized that he had been unaware of where he had been going or for how long he was gone. He walked along, disoriented, struggling to get his bearings and searching for anything familiar. There was no landmark that he could recognize. He was in unfamiliar territory, and waves of panic began to wash over the protective wall of Bernard's carefully constructed self-assurance. Where was he and how should he travel to get back home?

After a good bit of turning around, followed by a short, well-intended but hollow pep talk, self assurance was overrun and despair began to creep into Bernard's being. He was lost. He sat down and for the first time began to feel sorry for himself. How could all of this have happened to him? Oh, how he longed for the days when he walked through the competition day procession as an esteemed hero. As he looked around, those days began to feel as if they had completely slipped away. Here he was, lost and alone. And nothing he had learned could help him work his way out of the situation he found himself in.

Exhausted from the stress, Bernard sat down on the ground among the roots of a large oak tree. He let his eyes wander upward through the massive structure of the tree's branches and leaves accented with small patches of blue sky. From this perspective it seemed as if the branches of the tree were trying to stretch to the heavens for enlightenment. He envied the tree's stretch for the heights, and the stability and longevity the tree represented. He found comfort in its being and as he leaned his back against it, he felt warmth emanating from the trunk's bark. At a time when everything was in chaos in his life, sitting at the base of the tree made Bernard feel more secure. He closed his eyes, let his mind drift and tried to absorb the moment. It was almost as if the tree and the forest had something to say to him. Bernard's body began to relax, his mind calmed, and he drifted into a deep sleep.

As he slept, he dreamed. His dreams were of happy times filled with sweet confections. In this dream state he noticed that he felt lighter and more creative – just as he did in the early years of his career when he was learning, trying new things and developing relationships with his first customers. A warm, happy glow bathed his being. A sense of contentment filled Bernard – a feeling he hoped would never end.

Five

Suddenly, the loud snap of a breaking twig burst that warm glow and startled him awake. Bernard's reflexes coiled his body into a protective cowl. He opened his eyes to see a strange figure peering at him from a distance of about four feet. The figure stood no more than three feet high. It was a man – of sorts. At least it had the appearance of a man – two legs, two arms, two eyes, and a weathered face with a grayish beard. On top of his head was a pointed hat. The figure wore furry boots and his pants and coat caused one to think that he lived closely with the natural elements of the forest. In spite of his strange appearance he did not frighten Bernard; rather he felt compassion in the stranger's eyes and his demeanor.

"Who are you?" Bernard sheepishly inquired.

"Perhaps it is I who should be asking: Who are you?" replied the stranger.

After pausing to further check his surroundings and finding that he was still under the tree in the forest and that he and the stranger were the only ones present, Bernard began to regain his composure. He said, "I am a lost soul wandering and looking for answers."

Noticing that his answer increased the furrow in the little man's brow, he added, "I am Bernard. In Fredonia, I am referred to as the King's Baker ... or at least I was known by that recognition."

The little man stroked his ample beard with his hand and walked around to size up Bernard. "Fredonia? We have heard stories of a faraway place by that name. Hmm, a lost soul ... and a baker you say. What is a baker doing in the forest? And a king's baker at that? How can a soul be lost? ... and what on earth are you looking for so far from home?"

"I didn't plan on being far from Fredonia. I just started walking. ... I lost track of time, and the next thing

I knew I was here … lost."

"How can you be lost, for y   little man.

"Where exactly is here?" in

"Here is wherever you are. For you, here is in a great forest under the stately oak tree. … But never mind this circle of logic we find ourselves trapped in. What is a king's baker looking for in the forest?"

"Answers. … Insights. … Wisdom. You see I seem to have lost what it takes to be the King's Baker. Each year my famous torte had won the baking competition – but for the last several years it has lost out – dropping lower each year. I wanted to clear my head, so I took a walk … and wound up here."

"Of course. Now I understand," the little fellow said.

"What is it you understand? Please tell me because I understand none of this," Bernard replied.

"It is fortune that brings you here," said the fellow. "The spirit of the Great Baker has led you to me. You see, I am Harald the Baker, the most renowned baker in

st. I learned from the Great Baker, and his spirit
es me to this day. You were meant to be here."

"You look tired, thirsty and hungry. Follow me.
I'll take care of your needs, and as we walk, tell me
about your situation. And tell me why you make the
same torte when there are so many other wonders to
satiate the palette."

Bernard began to relax. In a surprising way he
began to trust this strange little man. As they walked
along he explained his situation to Harald. Now hav-
ing a bit of distance from his situation, he too began to
ask himself why he had stayed with the torte instead of
trying something else. Suddenly, a piece of information
he had quickly dismissed from the past resurfaced with
a whole new sense of importance. He had always been
quick to dismiss rumors. In a moment of sudden awareness Bernard realized that he was quick to do so because
the potential of rumors was often disruptive to what he
knew and was comfortable with. It just always seemed
to create a greater sense of control when he could stay
within the known, rather than drifting into wondering

about the possibilities of every piece of information that disrupted his sense of being.

He had heard this resurfaced piece of information often, but his concentration on the torte made it easy to dismiss. It was frequently mentioned in his bakery that the word in Fredonia was that Princess Madeline had gained significant status in the judging of the annual competition. It was also told that she advocated for the changing tastes of the younger generation of Fredonians and for those who were looking for breaks from tradition to a worldlier sampling of baked goods. Just as when the curtain is drawn back to reveal a stunning play scene, Bernard was knocked off balance by this resurfaced information and he began to perceive with a whole new sense.

As they moved along, more and more little people appeared from behind trees, rocks and underbrush. Bernard was stunned to realize they had been there all along, but they were so good at blending in and moving with the rhythm of the forest that they were undetectable to the untrained eye. Here in the forest, there was an entire culture of forest gnomes, as Bernard had discovered in his conversation with Harald.

That was not all Bernard learned. Once they arrived at Harald's village, Bernard learned more about this gnome clan's culture. And what an interesting culture this was. Harald told Bernard that his ancestors were once known for their furniture-making skills. Hard times caused the clan to adapt their lives to one of baking many years ago when the market for new furniture began to dry up. Because gnomes live for hundreds of years, holding on to their belongings for life and passing them on down family lines, the need for carpentry had diminished over the years and a new way of life was needed to sustain their families.

Their niche in the forest economy became supplying exquisite baked goods. It was a niche that this group of gnomes had defined and dominated for many years. The baking tradition in Harald's clan was in developing recipes to support the health and well-being of gnomes living in diverse communities throughout the forest. He caught Bernard's attention when Harald explained that shifting from furniture-making to baking was not an easy, clean or smooth transition. That transformation had been turbulent and gut-wrenching. Losing their identity as furniture-makers was something that Bernard's clan fought to hold on to for a long time. Some never did transition to the new identity, but eventually clan members made the shift as baking became more relevant for their survival. Now, clan members can't imagine themselves as anything but bakers. But they are very aware of adapting their baking techniques to the changing needs of their customers. They believe it is better to be open constantly for small adaptations rather than the alternative their ancestors faced. Their ancestors were not attuned to changing trends around them, and they were left to deal with a profound struggle for survival.

If ever there was a group that understood what it takes to make opportunity out of threat, this was it. The more they talked, the more Bernard felt that he could learn something from Harald, and that maybe it was fate after all that had brought them together.

Six

Harald brought Bernard a wonderful tasting, full-bodied drink and a splendid sampling of breads to settle a hunger Bernard had not realized he had. The two sat at tiny benches in a small clearing in the forest. All around them was the activity of the industrious gnome clan. As busy as they were, each gnome took the time for a greeting and warm welcome as he passed by.

The two bakers became involved in an engaging conversation about all sorts of things related to baking. It was a deeply reflective and stimulating dialogue – the type that comes around ever so rarely. It was an exchange that allowed Bernard to suspend his judgments and examine his thinking from a broader perspective. He had

" When is it time to get better...
and when is it time to become
different? "

heard the term "in the zone" used to describe the performance of the greatest knights as they jousted. Surely, this is what it must be like to be so focused and aware, yet relaxed and open. It was the type of experience one wants to hold on to and never relinquish – time seems to be absent on such occasions.

At one point of the dialogue, Bernard spoke of his driving desire to make the best torte. He spoke of how intensely he felt the need to not only make his recipe better and better, but in fact how compelled he was to be the best. After the comment Harald was silent for what seemed like a long time. In any other conversation it would have made Bernard uncomfortable. But not today, for Bernard knew that Harald was gathering his thoughts.

After taking a swig of the full-bodied drink, Harald spoke, "When is it time to get better… and when is it time to become different?"

He paused a moment to let his question sink in to Bernard's consciousness continued, "That is something we ask ourselves often. You see, getting better, improving our baked goods and how we bake them, is critical to our success. Yet, improvement works best when the conditions around us are stable – in other words when the tastes of the customers are predictable. But you have told me that the tastes of the judges, and perhaps your customers, are not as predictable as they used to be. So your efforts may be focused on working to get better at something that is losing its importance. That is why improving your recipe is not always good enough. In times like those you are experiencing, we find that becoming different is every bit as important as it is to get better. But it takes a different kind of leadership skill for a baker to help his bakery become different than it does to help it become better."

Harald's words caused Bernard to think about his situation in a way he had not in the past. The judges' tastes were changing, something he had not accounted for while he was focused on fixing his torte production. Bernard asked Harald to continue his thoughts.

Harald added, "Getting better requires bakers to value certainty and standardization, whereas becoming different means we need to rely on ambiguity and not knowing. This uncertainty is needed so that old ways can be questioned and released when necessary so that new ways can be adopted. We find that we open up to innovating when we find old ways of doing things aren't getting the results we want. It is times like this when not knowing is more important for the head baker than knowing. Letting go of old ways and leaping to new ones is vital to survival, but it is risky and unsettling. The difficulty is that we are never sure right away what new ways will work the best. So we have to enter a period of trying untested ideas. We much prefer times when things are stable and predictable, but we have learned how to manage our bakery so we move in to these periods of uncertainty and welcome them as an opportunity to renew ourselves rather than perceiving them as something awful that we should avoid at all cost. That change in perspective has really influenced how we organize and train our bakers, and it has been the most defining element of our success."

Harald's words resonated within Bernard and opened his eyes to an aspect of leadership that was unfamiliar to him. He wanted to know more and asked Harald to tell him more about how to organize a bakery for becoming different, as well as better.

He absorbed everything Harald told him, explaining how their training for bakers started with learning what it means to be a baker – not with the intent of developing the skills yet, but what it means in the lives of others when a baker bakes, giving everything he or she has to the process. After that, trainees learned to listen. The idea was to help the trainees not to just listen with their ears, but to listen for small things that people say, and to what they don't say, in order to feel a connection in their heart to their needs and to the passion of being a baker.

When it came to running the bakery, Bernard found Harald's advice unsettling at first. Harald told him that to have a bakery that stays vital and continuously adapts to people's tastes, a baker needs to avoid conventional wisdom about running a bakery. Harald's advice challenged what Bernard had learned from his studies at the Royal Bakers Institute – the authority on all things baking in Fredonia. It took him some time, and he had Harald repeat his advice several times. But, eventually

Harald's words began to break apart Bernard's paradigm for running a bakery. He did not yet completely comprehend at a deep level of understanding all that Harald said, but he did know that his advice had struck a welcoming chord and that the breaking apart of old ways had created a space for the "aha" of new understanding to light Bernard's spirit.

However, much of Harald's sage wisdom seemed paradoxical to Bernard. While he was hungry to understand, he also found he was becoming more and more confused. Harald's methods of leading a bakery seemed to create an expectation of the head baker to be an authority that provided firm structure, yet at the same time required him to welcome not knowing and to provide freedom to those in the bakery. Harald would speak about the importance of certainty and doing things his way, yet then drive home the point that it was important for Bernard to welcome ambiguity and encourage others to develop their way. At one point Bernard confronted his confusion and asked Harald, "Much of what you say seems contradictory. How does anyone provide both

"Leading a bakery that is always adapting to new trends means a head baker has to deal with apparent paradoxes."

structure and freedom or be an authority, not knowing? This all seems impossible to me.

Harald responded, "Leading a bakery that is always adapting to new trends means a head baker has to deal with apparent paradoxes. What you are seeing is but the ends of a spectrum – pieces of a whole. The paradox is within you. Once you resolve the paradox within your thinking and perceptions – within the way you view the world – then they cease to be paradoxical and you will operate freely within the full spectrum of leadership. And your bakery will be a healthy, thriving, living entity." His answer was something Bernard never forgot. It was something that he worked to fully understand the rest of his baking career.

Bernard knew that Harald's advice would start him on a new journey – a journey of unlearning, relearning and self-discovery. Bernard realized that instituting the concepts Harald had shared with him meant that he would feel like a novice for a while, and still he was excited and began to feel renewed. The journey of unlearning and relearning would not be easy, but he had never felt more

yet admit to
al-

> ❝ *Being a little off-balance is a healthy state because it prevents a baker and a bakery from being too rigid and too focused on the success of the past.* ❞

alive. Something deep inside had been awakened and while his leadership destination was uncertain and the road to get there might be difficult, Bernard was certain that he would grow and a new era of baking would fulfill him in ways he could not attain with his old methods.

Here is the conventional wisdom (leadership myths) to avoid that Harald relayed to Bernard:

MAINTAIN CONTROL AND STABILITY OF YOUR BAKING OPERATION AT ALL COST.

Being a little off-balance is a healthy state because it prevents a baker and a bakery from being too rigid and too focused on the success of the past. Little ripples of newness – new ideas, new information about taste trends, new ingredient combinations, or even ideas that threaten known methods – can help create openness to moving away from old recipes when their success is in its twilight or reinforce the need to stay with them when they are better than the new. Allowing people in the bakery to interact with and notice new and discordant information creates disturbances to the status quo. This is the way for a baker to develop a kitchen where creativity blossoms, and adaptability and innovation become what the bakery produces.

IN ORDER FOR A BAKERY TO BE EFFECTIVE AND EFFICIENT, STRATEGIES FOR WHAT TO BAKE NEED TO BE DEVELOPED BY THE HEAD BAKER.

Efficiency can be gained by this method of operation, yet when the head baker alone sets the direction for the bakery, the unique perspectives and talents of the assistant bakers are diminished. As a result, it is more likely for people to see their work as a job – something to perform rather than as work they feel connected to and passionate about. Instead, work to create a context for being that allows everyone to interpret and own it. Help the assistants understand what your bakery stands for and why it is important for everyone to understand and contribute his or her talents to that purpose. The more clearly understood and commonly held your bakery's purpose is, the less you need to direct strategies. Once you are sure that you continually help people relate to the meaning of that purpose, trust them to do what they think is right to accomplish it.

INFORMATION ABOUT RECIPES SHOULD BE CLOSELY GUARDED AND SHARED ONLY ON A NEED-TO-KNOW BASIS.

Information closely guarded and protected creates boundaries between levels of authority and perpetuates a belief that those highest up in the bakery are supposed to know more than those lower down. This method is acceptable when you are producing the same baked goods time after time and when the tastes of customers are constant; however, it is harmful for adaptability when tastes are changing and understanding those shifts is necessary for staying on top. Therefore, allow information to flow more freely through your bakery. Many eyes and ears interacting with it will create new perspectives. From that, new understanding about what the information means for your purpose will be generated. A head baker should not be the sole source for creative new recipes. Allow information to flow more freely, because you multiply exponentially the

You never know where the next great idea will come from, but it is there in your bakery waiting to come forward.

chance that a new recipe will be created. You never know where the next great idea will come from, but it is there in your bakery waiting to come forward.

A BAKERY WILL BECOME CHAOTIC AND INEFFICIENT UNLESS A HEAD BAKER IS THERE TO ORGANIZE THE WORKERS AND THEIR WORK.

This may be true for knights in battle, but it is not necessary for a bakery. Creating rigid structures to organize all of your bakery's work efforts is helpful for consistency and for maintaining the status quo, but it extinguishes innovation. Organizing production and assigning assistants to certain tasks is necessary, but who says you have to be the only one doing it?

Provide people the flexibility to interact with others and organize around their strengths. Allow assistants to connect with others and take on new challenges, recipes, and projects they feel passionate about. Who knows their strengths and passions better than they do? Give assistants from all over your bakery the chance to interact with others they might otherwise never talk to. In this way a new spark of potential is created with every

" Provide people the flexibility to interact with others and organize around their strengths. "

interaction. You just might find that your assistants self-organize into more highly productive relationships, with a greater sense of commitment to the product than what you could have ever created.

Seven

For the first time in a long time, Bernard felt the passion for baking touching his spirit. He was able to see the situation he had been in from a richer perspective. Bernard realized his strength was also his weakness (maybe he was beginning to perceive apparent paradoxes as pieces of the same whole after all). His famous torte created a foundation for his bakery, yet at the same time it had also become his weakness. The very thing that had brought him fame – the perfection of his torte – had also narrowed his focus and blinded him to other possibilities. Bernard noted that from now on he would try to see these concepts as part of the whole: seeking balance instead of pursuing one over the other.

Bernard began to think about his narrowed perspective; trying to find the right way had made him see baking as something to conquer instead of something to be a part of. He was suddenly saddened to think about how he had become someone who approached baking in a mechanical, analytical way, and in doing so he had lost contact with the needs of those around him and the art of baking. The change was so gradual he had not noticed it. He was embarrassed to say that in his mind he had become more important than the calling he had undertaken as a baker many years ago, and he vowed to reverse that. He paused a moment and spoke out loud a personal pledge for going forward: "I pledge to re-establish a bakery that nourishes the whole of all we serve as well as their appetites."

Harald spoke, "It sounds as if it is time to return to your bakery. I am honored that you found your way here and that we had the opportunity to talk to each other baker-to-baker."

"Harald, words cannot fully express my gratitude and admiration. You have rekindled within me the passion for baking and leading a bakery. I will be eternally grateful to you. I know I have a long way to go in fully understanding all you have told me, but I know that I see things differently now and will be persistent on my journey to become the leader of an adaptive, innovative bakery that thrives in a world of shifting taste trends," Bernard said.

"Being open to the journey is the first step. And you have taken it," Harald replied.

"Now, my cousin Joseph knows many secrets of the forest. He says he can lead you back to the slight tear in the boundaries between our worlds that you came through today," said Harald. "May your baking be the life's adventure all spirit's long for. And may our paths cross again. Good-bye my friend."

Bernard spoke a bit choked-up saying, "Good-bye my friend, and thank you."

Before long, Joseph had guided Bernard through twists and turns in the forest to a place where he could see a familiar path in a clearing just in front of him. He turned to thank Joseph, but he was nowhere to be seen.

Even the space in the underbrush he had just stepped through was no longer detectable. Bernard turned toward the now familiar route in front of him and headed for home with a quickened pace and a spring in his step. He could not wait to get to work.

As he moved along, Bernard's head was racing with thoughts of what to do when he got home. His feet seemed to fly, and the bakery was in sight before he knew it. He suddenly realized that he was unaware of what time it was. As a matter of fact, he was not even sure what day it was or for how long he had been gone. Would his assistants be at the bakery? What would they have been up to in his absence? He looked up and noticed that the sun was in an early-morning position in the sky.

"I wonder how many days I have been away?" he thought.

"At least it is morning and people will likely be at the bakery. I don't want to lose any more time," he said to himself. Bernard ran the rest of the way.

Bernard raced to the bakers' entrance in the back of the bakery. He throw open the door and with great excitement announced, "Hi, everybody. I'm back! I'm sorry I have been away so long, but I have some great news. I have a wonderful vision for our bakery and some great ideas I can't wait to tell you about. Let's get started ..." The startled expressions and open mouths looking at Bernard caused him to pause. The feeling of gloom in the room was palpable, and the body language of his assistants gave him the feeling that something horrible had happened. "What's wrong?" he asked. "What's going on? Is everyone all right?"

No one answered, they just stared at Bernard. Slowly and sheepishly his first assistant, Jacklyn, stepped forward and measured her words as she spoke. "What's wrong? You heard the announcement yesterday. We finished in fifth place. You were there. You heard it. We saw your reaction. We are all as devastated as you. If you fire all of us ... we understand. We have failed you."

After a moment, noticing a bewildered look on Bernard's face, assistant Claire added, "Are you okay? You seem ... well ... how can I say it ... so ...positive and up. That's not like you. ... I mean, that's not what any of us expected this morning."

> *... he had unintentionally created a bakery where people were dependent on him.*

"Yesterday? Oh that. The competition. Well, not much we can do about it now. ...What do you say we use that experience to help us become different, not just better?"

His employees seemed bewildered. Surely he was testing them. They knew that getting better was all that mattered.

Feeling he was holding his future in his hands, assistant Luke cautiously answered, "We know you are disappointed in us ... and we are disappointed in ourselves. We promise that we will work harder than ever and that we will commit everything we have to getting better. Please don't test our commitment – just tell us what to do."

A collective "Here, here," rumbled through the rest of the assembled workers. And then nodding heads and smatterings of "Yes, just tell us what to do," could be heard like a low wave moving through the group.

Bernard suddenly realized that the whole baking operation had been resting on his shoulders. He had been trying to instill certainty and confidence in his employees and in so doing, he had unintentionally created a bakery where people were dependent on him. He had been carrying the load for his entire bakery – no wonder he had felt so burdened. The joy of baking was absent in his employees. They were coming here to a job, and the way to stay secure in that job was to please the boss. "Your baking organization is not healthy," these words kept replaying themselves over and over in Bernard's head. All of what he had just experienced in the forest rushed back into his consciousness. Changes needed to start right away.

He spoke to his employees, "Look, I've had some time to think about what has happened. We could all spend time trying to fix blame and find fault with the judges, or the customers, or even with each other or with me. But that won't do us any good. I think it's time we looked at how we do things – how we know our customers and how we share ideas about baking and baked goods. What would you think if we started to think a little differently about how we do things? I've got some ideas I've been thinking about. It's going to take some time and we may experience some frustrations, because to do things differently we are going to have to unlearn some of what we've been doing and then relearn some better ways. But if we always remember why we're here – to please the palettes of the kingdom – then we can work through things together. What do you say? Shall we give it a go?"

The employees were silent at first. This change in Bernard's demeanor would take some getting used to, but they liked what they heard. Eventually, one clap lead to another and another until applause and cheering reverberated through the bakery.

Eight

Bernard began his journey that day. While his employees could see the need for change, the change was not easy. Bernard began to understand that people are for change until they are the ones who have to change. This was particularly evident as some of the practices began to challenge those established by the Baker's Guild. But Bernard knew that turning back was not the answer. He always found ways to muster the strength to move forward – and learned to turn threat into opportunity.

He started to spend more time and energy listening to people and relating their thoughts and ideas to the bakery's purpose. As the purpose became more alive within his people, principles for driving their work fol-

" involving everyone in the work of identifying problems and developing strategies to solve them increases the probability of an innovative spark "

lowed. These did not come from Berna
collective agreement of his employees.
purpose and principles formed a new w
the bakery.

Over time, Bernard began to see the work of his
employees in a new light. And with this, his expectations
of his employees began to change. Before his time with
Harald, he had thought of his employees' work in terms
of completing tasks. He had even thought of himself as
progressive in giving his employees a say in how things get
done by trying to involve them in decisions about completing those tasks. His time with Harald allowed him to
see that what he had really done was give them the chance
to be involved in technical fixes – improving what was already in place. He had not given them the chance to wres-
tle with the really challenging problems – the ones that
break new ground and create the next great recipe.

After his experience in the forest Bernard understood that great ideas can come from anywhere in the
bakery, not just from the top bakers. He realized that
involving everyone in the work of identifying prob-

s and developing strategies to solve them increases the probability of an innovative spark. So he expected his employees to begin to see potential problems before they materialized. He then expected them to be actively engaged in the sometimes messy process of creating new understanding from the void of not knowing.

How he organized people for work changed too. Bernard worked hard to break down barriers between employee groups and continually encouraged his workers to connect with each other in new ways. He also let the information in the organization flow more freely and allowed his people to organize around that information. On the whole once he was certain that people passionately understood the bakery's reason for being, he gave them the freedom to do what they thought was best to achieve that purpose.

While the direction of where he wanted to head was clear, the road was anything but smooth. There were often bumps and many times when Bernard just wanted to go back to jumping in and directing people, making decisions that seemed obvious to him – to just tell them what to do and how to do it. Every time he felt that urge, he thought back to the day of his return when everyone wanted him to tell them what to do. With that memory he knew that jumping in and fixing things was a short-term solution that in the end weakened people's ability to contribute.

Bernard stayed the course though there were many times he felt disoriented and lost. Unlearning was a difficult task, yet he realized it was the only way to stay relevant. In time he became more comfortable with the methods Harald had passed on to him that day when he wandered in the woods. What a fortunate, life-changing "wrong turn" that had been for him. He spent the rest of his days trying to master what he had learned. While he never felt he arrived as a master of the techniques, he did unlearn and relearn. In the end, he became much more capable of really leading his people – and his bakery continued to thrive, always seeming to come up with something new at just the right time.

The ability to do that was not blind luck. It had been a very humbling moment when Bernard had realized that he had focused only on improving his torte and had not connected the information about Princess Madeline's possible involvement and that the judges tastes were changing. Realizing how important it is to sort through lots of seemingly disconnected information to find the trend, Bernard worked to develop a connection with someone who saw the world differently – Princess Madeline. What began as a chance encounter eventually became a deep, respected friendship. Bernard valued greatly the Princess's insights into the taste trends of her people – particularly the younger Fredonians. She respected Bernard's ability to listen and interpret her insights. Later, when the Princess married and moved away from Fredonia, Bernard was able to develop a network of important acquaintances that helped him stay attuned to the pulse of Fredonia's taste trends.

Over the years, Bernard's bakery did not win every competition – but it did win more than its fair share. Bernard's reputation grew to be one of an innovator – a baker who understood the needs of the people and the changes in their taste, better than they did themselves.

His bakery could be counted on to hold tight to the best taste traditions, while at the same time, they were always filling the niche of a new trend ahead of anyone else.

As time passed, the King grew to count on Bernard as a trusted advisor. His admiration for Bernard and his bakery were enormous. He loved not only what they created, but how they did business – always out in front of a trend, connected to the needs of Fredonia. The King thought of Bernard's bakery as a model for the best Fredonians had to offer. His respect was so great that he awarded Bernard the official title, complete with all its prestige, grandeur, and royal perks: The King's Baker.

It should be told, however, that Bernard did hold on to some of his old ways. One of which was to not share his recipes. He did modify this to become not sharing recipes with those outside of his bakery. Yet, he did have one exception. Bernard's desire was to pass his learning on to others so that they may experience the fulfillment of leading others on a journey of continuous renewal and innovation. Here are his "recipes for success" passed on to you:

Help people focus on real work. The more you are able to establish clearly understood, commonly shared purpose and principles, the less you have to rely on command and control. When employees see their work as more than a job, they are more likely to do real work instead of pretend work.

Where you stumble, your treasure lies. As a matter of fact, one of the most important roles of a leader is to disturb the system rather than to make disturbances go away. When things go wrong, are incongruent or occur unexpectedly, they afford opportunity to break apart old ways and open the door for new approaches. Move into them, not away from them.

FROM THE KITCHEN OF:
Bernard, the King's Baker

Become comfortable in the zone between chaos and order (and help others to do so as well). It is where creativity, opportunity, renewal and sustainability lie. The key to working in this zone, is to help your organization never change (holding tight to key values and purpose), while helping it endlessly adapt (what those values and purpose mean should be constantly renewing).

Bernard, the King's Baker

Either/or is only half the story. Try to view your challenges as paradoxes for they open one to the "whole" of a situation. Working in this way affords greater opportunities for "out of the box" ideas to take root.

FROM THE KITCHEN OF:
Bernard, the King's Baker

You are a part of something larger. Participate with this: Doing good is better for longevity than is a profit-only motive.

Bernard, the King's Baker

Your strength can become your weakness. Do not let your vanity for past success isolate you from the world and its presence. Growing attached to and comfortable with the status quo hampers your ability to tap into creativity.

FROM THE KITCHEN OF:
Bernard, the King's Baker

Learn to listen ... and listen carefully. Be conscious of listening deeply; not only to what is being said, but also to how it is being said. What are the feelings and hopes underlying the message you are receiving? Seek out people's needs and expectations of you and your product and/or service. Then strive to meet those needs and, more importantly, work to exceed expectations. You will be surprised and pleased with what you discover by applying the skill of listening.

Bernard, the King's Baker

Look in the mirror to assess yourself as a leader before you blame others for their errors. You may find there is more to correct in your mental models and in the system than there is in the individual.

Bernard, the King's Baker

Let ideas collide – and remember that bottom-up often works better than top-down. Create the conditions for ideas to continually spark off each other, remix, create fusion, and either grow in strength or diminish. Make sure those ideas that rise to the surface have a chance to engage and compete against those driving existing practice.

From the Kitchen of:
Bernard, the King's Baker

Transformation is a journey. You may never quite arrive at the destination you imagine, but the point is that the process is in many ways more important than the product. By stepping on the path of a journey you begin the process of unlearning and relearning, seeing things in new and transforming ways. On this topic Bernard was known to say, "When I approached the fork in the road, I took the road less traveled and that has made all the difference." (With respect to Robert Frost who used similar words in his famous poem, The Road Not Taken – we, the authors, can only surmise that he must have borrowed the idea from his predecessor, Bernard.)

May the torte be with you.

Epilogue

There you have it. Even during Medieval times, Bernard and his staff faced that ever-persistent dynamic called change. In today's world, change is occurring at an ever-accelerating pace. Every organization faces what Bernard did: The pace of change is moving faster than the ability to adjust. With the availability and transfer of information and knowledge literally happening at the speed of light, it is little wonder that organizations struggle to stay abreast of change. Beyond that, today change itself has changed. It is no longer just about pace; the direction of change is often unpredictable. In today's connected world, small ripples in the distance can suddenly come from nowhere and turn into powerful waves that alter the course of an organization.

Under these conditions, organizational survival depends on constant assessment of and adjustment to changes in the external environment. For businesses and organizations, adaptation takes the form of innovation. It is important to keep in mind that innovation is far more than coming up with the next product line or profit-making idea. As Bernard discovered, it is about developing a new way of being: a new way of understanding your organizational identity, a new way of thinking about information and a new way of understanding relationships.

First and foremost, Bernard's story highlights the most important innovation you can make is to innovate the way you lead. This is a journey of adaptation and renewal that involves learning, unlearning and relearning. The journey starts when the tried-and-true methods of leadership are not providing the means for quick, adaptive responses to changes in the external environment. The first steps involve adapting your thinking about leadership from the success formulas derived from a command-and-control world to those better suited to an information-rich, individually empowered, self-organizing world. Once the leader's thinking changes, then and only then, can an organizational culture that supports innovation be shaped.

As Bernard found, to truly create an innovative organization, the leader must take an inner journey that involves letting go of old ways so that new, more potent understandings can guide his or her leadership. For Bernard, the first step on the journey was an internal reframing of the situation; the meaning of his relationship to the external changes needed to be altered. However, such adjustments can mean old ways of thinking and doing must be left behind so new, more attuned ways can be developed. This is hard work for leaders because it means some of the things that have produced success in the past may be the very things that limit one's ability to stay successful.

Our intention in bringing this story to you is to offer you a new perspective on leading and shaping innovation within your organization. We want you to see the development of your skills as an innovative leader as a journey. On this journey the traditional experts cannot tell us what and how to do things. Their work tells us what practices have produced the best results, as based on past formulas for success. However, their expertise cannot tell us about the next practices – what works best under an evolving success formula. No one can tell us that because each situation is unique. When it comes to innovation an adaptive response tailored to your organization is required. While there is a void of expert advice, fortunately, just as with the sage advice Bernard received, there are some principles that can guide you on your journey.

• Incorporate dissonance into your leadership repertoire – Develop sensitivity to disturbances. Notice information that is discordant with your current state – and move into it, not away from it.

• Work to clarify your organizational identity – In turbulent times identity is what brings order out of chaos. Consciously work to illuminate a clear, coherent identity that is a continuous reference for creating meaning to new information, one where everyone knows why they are there and one that allows individuals the freedom to act within that purpose to better the organization.

- Change your awareness to where solutions lie – Instead of looking for outside experts, become more aware of the latent potential within your organization. Use the challenges you face to adapt by developing internal capacities to solve key problems.

- Encourage the interaction of ideas – Work to foster a climate where ideas can percolate, grow in importance and interact with the existing order. Shape a culture where "we have not arrived" is celebrated. Encourage the conditions for new responses to become the new norm – for the old ways to be replaced by new ways.

The "how to" for the work of creating an innovative organization is unique to every individual and organization, but the path for this journey has been shown to us. It is one that has been followed for centuries by those of character: Depart a familiar state to travel in a place of challenge and not knowing, to gain insights and understanding that gives one new potency, and then to bring that new understanding to life by making the lives of those around us better. To open the door to your journey, we leave you with some questions to ponder and hope that wonder leads you on:

- Can you as leader accept that innovative ideas will not necessarily come from the top?

- Can you deal with the idea that dissonance, disturbance and ambiguity are your allies, not something to be quashed, stabilized and immediately explained so you can get on with "business"?

- Can you trust that the key innovative ideas dwell in the areas of uncertainty and perceived impossibility? Can you accept that such ideas are probably not accepted "best practices"?

- Can you recognize an innovation when it stares you in the face, hides in the periphery of your organization or is presented inarticulately?

- How does an innovative organization behave in the face of ambiguous data and information? How does the leader behave?

- Can you let new information change your perceptions, rather than changing the information so it fits your already held perceptions? Are you willing to "let ideas collide" at the same time as you build a coherent, collectively held, and deeply motivating identity and set of values that those in the organization support to the very core of their being?

• Can you accept that order and structure in an innovative environment has to emerge from the organization itself, and NOT be imposed by the strength or force of the leader's personality and mandates "from the top"? Can you, as a leader of your organization, accept that innovation and an innovative culture cannot be mandated... it can only be provoked, grown, nurtured?

About the Authors

ROBERT DAVIDOVICH ED.D. is an assistant professor in the School of Leadership at Cardinal Stritch University. He is the founder of Leading for Innovation Associates, LLC, serving as a consultant specializing in transformational change, innovation, systems thinking, and organizational development. He is lead author of the book, Beyond School Improvement: The Journey to Innovative Leadership, published by Corwin Press.

JOHN KOEHN PH.D. is a consultant and facilitator of strategic planning. He works with both private and public organizations on topics dealing with innovative leadership, total quality management techniques, and conflict resolution strategies. He is a retired teacher and school administrator and has been an adjunct professor on the faculties of the University of Wisconsin-Milwaukee and Cardinal Stritch University.

11690116R0007

Made in the USA
Lexington, KY
25 October 2011